# PRAY IT OUT

## 40 DAYS OF CASTING YOUR CARES ON JESUS

AN INTERACTIVE DEVOTIONAL

KATY McCOWN

AMEN

# Contents

# Introduction

**I LISTENED AS ONE OF MY KIDS SHARED THE CONCERNS OF THEIR HEART.** This particular child had worked hard, tried to honor others, and tried even harder to be patient, yet still felt unseen and unappreciated.

As I listened, my thoughts swirled with all of the possible ways I could respond.

We could have tried to *figure it out.* I could have offered to *talk it out.* I might have even tried to get involved and *work it out.* At the very least, I could have encouraged my child to *wait it out.*

But it occurred to me: I actually didn't want any of those options for my bewildered youth. So I offered something else instead: I silenced the swirl of thoughts in my mind and said, *Let's pray it out.*

From that point on, every time my child felt frustrated, anxious, or confused about the situation, we knew what to do—pray. We didn't get our answers immediately. In fact, it took weeks of praying it out before we saw things begin to change. But we did see God's activity in the situation, and we knew without a doubt it was His faithfulness and His provision at work.

I've found that, just like when I tried to help my child, many times when we're faced with uncertain or overwhelming circumstances, we are inclined to try to figure it out, work it out, or at the very least, wait it out—but the end result is often the same: We live drained from carrying the mental, emotional, and physical demands of trying to handle it all.

If that's you, I want to encourage you—you're not alone. One recent study, conducted over a three-month period, reported that more than one in five women between the ages of eighteen and forty-four felt exhausted most days.[1] In another study, nearly half of women said they felt drained.[2]

The great news is that since we are followers of Jesus, God provides us with another option . . . we can *pray it out.*

Each day of this prayer devotional will include a Scripture, bite-sized devotional, guided prayer, and practical reflection questions. I hope this book gives you words to whisper when you don't know where to begin. I pray it becomes something you reach for when you need to remember that God has it all under control. As you do, I pray you will live energized by God's presence instead of exhausted from carrying the weight of the world.

1. https://www.cdc.gov/mmwr/volumes/72/wr/mm7245a7.htm#:~:text=In%20 2022%2C%2013.5%25%20of%20adults,men%20in%20each%20age%20group

2. https://www.cnbc.com/2023/03/14/burnout-is-on-the-rise-gen-z-millennials-and-women-are-the-most-stressed.html#:~:text=Published%20Tue%2C%20Mar%2014%202023,burn-out%20than%20men%20(37%25)

DAY 1

# A Prayer When You Need to Quiet Your Fears

*When I consider your heavens, the work of your fingers, the moon and the stars, which you have set in place, what is mankind that you are mindful of them, human beings that you care for them?*
**Psalm 8:3-4 (NIV)**

**SOMETIMES IT FEELS LIKE EACH DAY BRINGS A NEW ONSLAUGHT OF CHAOS INSIDE MY MIND.** My responsibilities, the needs and feelings of my people, and my decisions fall one on top of another, leaving me worried and weary.

If you're like me, you may have quietly asked yourself this question: *If I don't figure all of this out, who will?* Psalm 8 helps us find the answer.

David wondered about who God is and why He would choose to consider the human race at all. In doing so, he also noted two truths: God thinks about us, and God cares for us.

Because God has us on His mind, we can take our burdens off of our minds. Not only can we take all of our things off our minds, but Psalm 8 also gives us something to replace those thoughts with—our Lord.

But note the necessary process of placing and keeping our minds on God:

> *"When I consider your heavens, the work of your fingers, the moon and the stars, which you have set in place . . ."* **(Psalm 8:3)**

David did not just glance at God. He didn't even pause to simply acknowledge God. The Hebrew word in this passage translated "consider" can also be defined as "inspect" or "look intently at."

Our nature steers us to believe we couldn't possibly trade our worldly concerns for moments to sit and think about God. But when we feel like that, we can remember that because God has us on His mind, we are free to give our attention to who He is and allow His character to quiet our fears.

## PRAY

**Dear God, I don't want to waste one more day smothered by my deafening thoughts. They steal my attention from the beauty of Your majesty, and I miss Your glory all around me. Quiet my soul, I pray. May today be the beginning of a new thought pattern in my life. Let Your joy fill my soul as I think of You. In Jesus' name, Amen.**

## REFLECT

WHAT FEARS ARE STIRRING IN YOUR SOUL TODAY?

USE THE SPACE BELOW TO WRITE DOWN SOME OF THE THINGS THAT YOU KNOW ARE TRUE ABOUT GOD. IF YOU CAN'T THINK OF ANYTHING, CONSIDER ASKING A TRUSTED FRIEND, OR EVEN STEP OUTSIDE AND SIMPLY TAKE IN GOD'S CREATION ALL AROUND YOU. WHAT DOES GOD'S CREATION REVEAL ABOUT HIS CHARACTER?

WHAT IS ONE THING YOU CAN DO TODAY TO SHIFT YOUR ATTENTION FROM YOUR FEARS TO THE MAJESTY AND POWER OF GOD?

DAY 2

# A Prayer When It Feels Like Life Is Spinning Out of Control

*He [Jesus] got up, rebuked the wind and said to the waves, "Quiet! Be still!" Then the wind died down and it was completely calm.*
**Mark 4:39 (NIV)**

**SCRIPTURE GIVES US SEVERAL EXAMPLES OF JESUS' CONTROL OVER ALL THINGS.** One of my favorite examples is in Mark's Gospel, where we see Jesus' control over the wind and the sea (**Mark 4:35-41**).

As the waves of the sea crashed into the boat, Jesus' disciples woke Him with a question: ". . . do you not care that we are perishing?" (**Mark 4:38b**).

Based on what they perceived through the lens of their human eyes, Jesus' disciples expected great loss. They even wondered if Jesus cared. However, after Jesus quieted the storm, the disciples asked, "Who then is this, that even the wind and the sea obey him?" (**Mark 4:41**).

Jesus' demonstration of His control over creation brought His disciples to a deeper understanding of His power and authority.

While we are sure to encounter storms in life, when we ponder the completeness of Jesus' victory and the vastness of His control, it helps us live by faith instead of shrinking back in fear (**Mark 4:40; Hebrews 10:39**).

When we see our circumstances through the lens of Jesus' control, we find the confidence to continue. Because of Jesus, not only can we endure hardships but we can also rejoice in them, certain of the future that has been placed under His feet alone.

## PRAY

**Heavenly Father, today when I face trials and tribulations, help me remember Your authority. When I look at the sun, feel the wind on my face, and watch the birds of the air, let me recall Your care and control over all things. As I do, may I not only endure but may I also rejoice in the certain and coming reign of Jesus. In Jesus' name, Amen.**

## REFLECT

HOW DOES YOUR PERSPECTIVE ON YOUR CURRENT CIRCUMSTANCES SHAPE WHAT YOU EXPECT TO HAPPEN NEXT?

HOW DOES THE CONTRAST BETWEEN JESUS' PERSPECTIVE IN THE STORM AND THE DISCIPLES' PERSPECTIVE HELP YOU SEE YOUR CIRCUMSTANCES THROUGH A LENS OF FAITH RATHER THAN FEAR?

THINK ABOUT THE DAY AHEAD AND SCHEDULE A TIME TO STEP OUTSIDE, PRAY, AND REMEMBER GOD'S CONTROL (EVEN IF IT'S JUST FOR FIVE MINUTES). WHEN AND WHERE WILL YOU DO THIS?

DAY 3

# A Prayer for God to Equip You for What's Ahead

*Whatever happens, conduct yourselves in a manner worthy of the gospel of Christ . . . stand firm in the one Spirit, striving together as one for the faith of the gospel.*
**Philippians 1:27 (NIV)**

A FEW YEARS AGO, I WENT ON A PRE-DAWN HIKE WITH THE WHOLE FAMILY. To see the sunrise from the mountain peak we began our ascent at 3 a.m., to be exact.

The hike was seven miles round trip and started out as a fun family adventure. It was almost as though we didn't notice how early it was or how long the trail would be.

When we began our trip up the mountain, we spread out a little on the trail. Some of the kids went at a faster pace. Others took their time. After several hours of hiking, though, we grew tired, hungry, and weary, and things changed.

Instead of going at our own pace, we stayed closer to each other. We knew we needed each other, so we stuck together.

Believe it or not, we made it up the mountain, watched the sunrise, and then made it all the way back down. Later that morning, after a few cups of coffee and a hot breakfast, I thought more about what had transpired on our hike.

Here's what I learned: We won't always know when the journey of life will become difficult, but when it does, who is traveling with us will become very important. As we ask God to equip us for what's ahead, let's remember to fix our eyes on Jesus and walk in Him. Let's also be on the lookout for those He may lead us to walk with.

## PRAY

**Dear Heavenly Father, fill me with the knowledge of Your will in all wisdom and spiritual understanding so that I may walk worthy of the Lord and fully pleasing to You. Equip me for what's ahead so that I will bear fruit in every good work and grow in the knowledge of God. Strengthen me according to Your glorious might so that I may have great endurance and patience, joyfully giving thanks to the Father. In Jesus' name, Amen. (Colossians 1:9-12)**

## REFLECT

WHERE ARE YOUR EYES FIXED?
ON THE FUTURE OR ON JESUS?

HOW CAN YOU POSITION YOURSELF FOR GOD TO BRING PEOPLE INTO YOUR LIFE TO WALK WITH YOU AND ENCOURAGE YOU IN CHRIST?

DAY 4

# A Prayer to Help You Live Expectantly

*Whatever you do, do it from the heart, as something done for the Lord and not for people.*
**Colossians 3:23 (CSB)**

**YEARS AGO, MY FAMILY PILED INTO THE CAR AFTER A LONG FOOTBALL SEASON AND LOOKED FORWARD TO THE PLACE WE CALLED HOME.** We hit the road before sunrise, and my then-pregnant self snuggled up with a pillow in the passenger seat . . . right up until the time my husband pulled off for an unscheduled stop.

I sat up, annoyed, and demanded to know the reason for the change in our schedule. This would surely throw our time of arrival way off. With a huff and a scowl, I stomped into the gas station. That's when I encountered a kind man who changed my day.

Mopping the floor in front of the door, the man greeted me with a smile and a "Good morning."

His kindness stopped me (and my bad attitude) in my tracks. He, too, was up at sunrise—not on his way home, but at work, mopping the well-worn floor of the gas station. Yet he did it with a smile and with a heart that cared to share that smile.

His example gives me hope for the impact of the simplest task when we do it for the Lord.

At the time I write this, it has been more than fifteen years since my path crossed his that day in the early-morning hours. I'm sure he never would have guessed how much his smile and kind words would impact a woman in the trenches of everyday life.

When we offer our daily routines to the Lord and allow His heart to influence everything we do, we can live expecting God to do more than we could imagine with even the simplest action of love in service to Him.

## PRAY

**Heavenly Father, it's exciting to imagine what You can do with the things that feel small in my life. Change my heart so that I approach every detail of my day as service to You. Help me not dismiss anything as unimportant or unusable by You. As I serve You with spiritual fervor today, give me a glimpse of Your great plans being worked out all around me. In Jesus' name, Amen.**

## REFLECT

WHAT ARE SOME OF YOUR DAILY TASKS THAT FEEL MUNDANE OR UNIMPORTANT?

HOW WILL YOU CHANGE YOUR APPROACH TO THESE TASKS TODAY SO THAT YOU DO THEM EXPECTANTLY AND WITH ALL OF YOUR HEART?

DAY 5

# A Prayer When You Need to Remember God Is with You

*Fear not, for I am with you; be not dismayed,*
*for I am your God; I will strengthen you, I will help you,*
*I will uphold you with my righteous right hand.*
**Isaiah 41:10**

**IN TODAY'S VERSE, GOD MADE TWO STATEMENTS TO HIS CHILDREN:**

*I am with you.*
*I am your God.*

Because of these two facts, the children of God were promised three things:

*He will strengthen, help, and uphold us with His righteous right hand.*

I'm smiling as I type. What great promises we have from our God! But it gets better! Three verses later in Isaiah 41, God said this:

> *For I, the Lord your God, hold your right hand; it is I who say to you, "Fear not, I am the one who helps you"* **(Isaiah 41:13).**

Once again, we read about how God helps His people, and therefore we do not need to fear. We also read about God's right hand. This time, though, it is our own right hand that God is holding.

Coupled with verse 10, this paints the picture of God as the loving Father He is—holding your right hand with His left hand and going before you with His righteous right hand to guard, defend, and help you.

I pray this beautiful picture of God's love and support brings you rest and hope today.

## PRAY

**Dear God, thank You for the promise that You are with me. Today, I turn to You to receive help and strength in my time of need. I give You my right hand to hold firmly in Your grip. Help me not to be afraid as You go before me. In Jesus' name, Amen.**

## REFLECT

DESCRIBE A TIME YOU WALKED HAND IN HAND WITH SOMEONE. WHO WAS IT? WHERE WERE YOU GOING? HOW DID YOU FEEL? HOW DID THEY FEEL?

WHAT THOUGHTS COME INTO YOUR MIND WHEN YOU CONSIDER THE IMAGE OF GOD HOLDING YOUR HAND, LEADING YOU AND HELPING YOU?

WHAT IS ONE THING YOU NEED HELP WITH TODAY? WRITE THE DETAILS IN THE BLANKS BELOW, AND THE NEXT TIME YOU ENCOUNTER THIS SITUATION, LET IT BE A REMINDER TO PRAY.

**DAY 6**

# A Prayer to Prepare You for Today

*Those who drink the water I give will never be thirsty again. It becomes a fresh, bubbling spring within them, giving them eternal life.*
**John 4:14 (NLT)**

**YEARS AGO, I LISTENED TO SOMEONE DESCRIBE WHAT MY LIFE FELT LIKE EVERY DAY.** "Women live like a cup tipped over on its side," they said. "They pour and pour and pour out, but they never refill."

The person went on to share a different picture, though. This time, instead of a cup on its side, they told of a cup sitting right-side up. Instead of a cup emptied, this cup sat beneath a constant stream of water.

The water still poured out into the space around it, but it was the result of an overflow of what was being poured into the cup.

When we rely on ourselves to handle everything the day brings, we live like that empty cup. We pour out our energy, strength, and emotions, but we never seem to fill back up. Day after day we pour out, and eventually we run out.

But we have another option. We can shift every burden to God's capable hands—the ones we know are coming, and the ones that surprise us.

We don't know what each day holds, but God sees what's next. He knows what we need and how to equip us for the things ahead. When we bring our day to Him, we will face the same obstacles and demands, but instead of drawing from our own reservoir of resources, we will receive everything we need from Jesus' stream of living water.

## PRAY

**Dear God, Thank You for Your faithfulness to fill me up. I want to abide in You today. Alert me when I start to rely on my own strength or resources, and remind me that it is You who works in me to work out Your purposes. Help me remain in You and rely on You alone for everything I need. In Jesus' name, Amen.**

## REFLECT

WHAT ARE YOU TRYING TO DO USING YOUR OWN STRENGTH TODAY?

WHY DOES IT FEEL LIKE YOU
DON'T HAVE TIME TO SIP FROM JESUS'
SPRING OF LIVING WATER?

HOW WILL YOU PREPARE
DIFFERENTLY FOR TODAY TO REMAIN IN
CHRIST AND RECEIVE HIS PROVISION?

DAY 7

# A Prayer When You Need Comfort

*Even when I go through the darkest valley, I fear no danger, for you are with me; your rod and your staff—they comfort me.*
**Psalm 23:4 (CSB)**

**IT STARTED LIKE A NORMAL TRIP TO WALMART . . .** as normal as you get with six kids in tow.

We made it up and down a few grocery aisles before the business of my little tribe became more than I felt I could handle, so I abandoned the list entirely and declared that the shopping trip was over. About that time, we heard hail pounding so loud on the roof that my three-year-old covered his ears. I prayed as we walked toward the door, hoping it wasn't as bad as it sounded, only to find out that a "weather alert" required every shopper to move to the center of the store.

With a smile and an "Okay," my caravan turned in the other direction. And I can't explain it, but in the midst of this literal whirlwind, peace ruled.

The two kids who spent most of the morning pushing and poking each other now sat side by side in the cart without a word or a shove. My oldest son, who normally needs to know why I ask him to do anything, followed behind me, pushing a loaded-down cart, without a question.

As we stood next to the fitting rooms, we all started to sing a song from my childhood: "He's got the wind and the rain in His hands. He's got the wind and the rain in His hands . . . He's got the whole world in His hands."

By the time we finished the song, we were told that it was safe to leave. As we entered the parking lot and surveyed the still-ominous sky, a stranger offered to help me load kids and groceries into the car.

That day I saw God's fingerprints in the midst of the literal storm. God doesn't always hold back the storm, but He will always walk us through it, comforting, providing, and guiding us.

## PRAY

**Oh Lord, You are my Shepherd who comforts me. In You, I have all that I need. Bring me to rest in green pastures. Lead me beside quiet waters. Refresh and restore my soul. Even when I walk through the valley of the shadow of death, I will not fear. Let Your protection and guidance bring me comfort today. In Jesus' name, Amen.**

## REFLECT

WHAT STORM ARE YOU WALKING THROUGH TODAY?

ASK GOD TO SHOW YOU HOW HE HAS BEEN PRESENT WITH YOU IN THE MIDST OF YOUR TRIAL. RECORD WHAT HE REVEALS IN THE SPACE BELOW.

DAY 8

# A Prayer to Help You Turn to God in Times of Trouble

*Now, O Lord our God, save us, please, from his hand, that all the kingdoms of the earth may know that you, O Lord, are God alone.*
**2 Kings 19:19 (ESV)**

**MY HUSBAND HAD BEEN GONE FOR SEVERAL WEEKS, WHICH LEFT ME FULLY RESPONSIBLE FOR OUR SIX CHILDREN.** When he returned home and began to unpack his things, he caught a glimpse of my "in case of emergency" plan.

"Katy," he said, "why is there a can of hair spray and a T-ball bat next to your bed?"

Should an intruder enter the house, I figured I'd blind him with the hair spray then smack him with the bat. It seemed foolproof to me, but my husband didn't agree.

In the book of 2 Kings, we meet a king who wasn't just preparing in case of emergency but who found himself fully immersed in one. King Hezekiah stood firm in the face of his enemy because he knew God and believed what he had heard about Him. (You can read all about it in **2 Kings 19:1-36**.)

The same God who paved the way to deliver Hezekiah has made a way for us too. Only One is able to deliver us. His name is Jesus. He is able, He is faithful, and in Him all nations can put their hope (**Matthew 12:21**).

The strength of our deliverer will determine whether we stand or surrender to our enemy. God is able to deliver us and is faithful to keep His promises. When we trust Him, we will turn to Jesus daily for deliverance from sin and the schemes of Satan.

When we don't, we will look for another deliverer—sometimes our own good works or maybe the wisdom and strength of man. But both of these options are as sure to save us as my can of hair spray and T-ball bat.

## PRAY

**Dear God, show me my faulty fortresses. Expose the moments in my life when I turn to a deliverer other than You. Ground me in the truth that You alone can rescue me, and grant me hope as I trust in You as my Deliverer. In Jesus' name, Amen.**

## REFLECT

WHAT OR WHO ARE YOU INCLINED TO TURN TO IN TIMES OF TROUBLE OTHER THAN GOD?

HOW HAVE YOU SEEN
THESE FAULTY FORTRESSES FAIL IN
YOUR TIME OF NEED?

WHAT DO YOU THINK KEEPS
YOU FROM TURNING TO AND TRUSTING
IN GOD COMPLETELY?

DAY 9

# A Prayer When You Want to Walk in Your Calling

*If anyone cleanses himself from what is dishonorable he will be a vessel for honorable use, set apart as holy, useful to the master of the house, ready for every good work.*
**2 Timothy 2:21 (ESV)**

**HER QUESTION CAUGHT ME OFF GUARD A LITTLE, AS I PONDERED MY REPLY.** No one had ever asked me this question before.

After teaching at a women's conference for aspiring writers and speakers, a woman posed the question to me: "When did you start teaching the Bible?" And for the life of me, I couldn't remember.

As I searched my memory for that first moment of teaching the Bible (and likely took longer to answer the question than expected), I landed on the answer that came as a surprise, even to me.

I started teaching the Bible not on a stage or even in a church. I first taught the Bible sitting on the floor in my kids' bedroom. My first teaching likely lasted two minutes, since my children were young and their attention spans matched their ages. But one night at a time, one year at a time, we sat down together and opened the Bible.

At that moment, I wondered—would I ever have taught the Bible in other settings if I hadn't first taught it there, in a place unseen by most, with results that were as unseen as that place? Yet this was the scene of my first calling.

God always knows what we need to follow His calling. To walk in our callings today is actually very simple. All we have to do is serve our Caller.

# PRAY

**Dear God, I want my life to bring You glory. Help me get rid of anything in my behavior that is offensive to You. There is no sin that is worth forfeiting my calling. Let me continually remember that I was bought with the precious blood of Christ, and let that compel me to have no higher priority than being Your servant. In Jesus' name, Amen.**

# REFLECT

WHAT IS SOMETHING YOU BELIEVE GOD HAS CALLED YOU TO DO?

WHAT DO YOU NEED TO CLEANSE YOURSELF FROM
IN ORDER TO BE READY FOR THIS WORK AND
EVERY GOOD WORK GOD HAS FOR YOU?

HOW CAN YOU PRIORITIZE SERVING GOD RIGHT WHERE YOU ARE?

DAY 10

# A Prayer to Help You Follow God Today

*I will instruct you and teach you in the way you should go;*
*I will counsel you with my loving eye on you.*
**Psalm 32:8 (NIV)**

**WITH NO TIME TO SPARE, I BARRELED DOWN THE DRIVEWAY TOWARD MY SON'S WRITING CLASS.** Without warning, my van started giving directions. I had no idea where the voice was taking me or why she even started talking, but since all of my attempts to silence her failed, I listened to her give directions the whole way to class. The only problem was, I wasn't headed in the direction she wanted me to go.

After a few minutes, I figured out where the voice in my van insisted I go: home.

We were currently living in south Louisiana, but somehow the place we called "home base" in East Texas had been programmed into the navigation system in my van, and the voice behind the map kept telling me to go there. With every turn that didn't lead to Texas, she rerouted me. "Make a legal U-turn," she'd say—over and over and over.

I giggled at her persistence—and at the fact that I couldn't turn her off. She knew where she wanted me to go.

Wouldn't it be great if God's voice was that distinguishable in our lives? But sometimes our days get noisy. And in all our running around, we can miss God's voice instructing and counseling us.

Like the voice in my van, we keep going in our own direction—exhausted, overwhelmed, frustrated, and confused. All the while, God, like a spiritual navigator, relentlessly urges us to make a U-turn.

The truth is, there's really no such thing as not enough time. There is enough time in every day to accomplish God's purposes for that day. To follow God, maybe we just need to begin with one simple question: God, what do You want me to do today?

As we listen for His answer and follow His lead, we'll trade confusion for clarity, frustration for peace, and exhaustion for rest.

## PRAY

**Dear God, what do You want me to do today? I bring You my list of things to do and my plans for this day, and I ask You to arrange them according to Your will. Align my desires with Your direction. Lead me and guide me for Your name's sake, and by Your great grace let today be more fruitful than I could ever imagine. In Jesus' name, Amen.**

## REFLECT

WHAT RESISTANCE DO YOU FEEL ABOUT RELEASING YOUR PLANS TO THE LORD?

DO YOU BELIEVE THERE IS ENOUGH
TIME IN THIS DAY TO ACCOMPLISH GOD'S PLANS
FOR THE DAY? WHY OR WHY NOT?

ASK GOD TO SHOW YOU ANY DESIRES OF YOUR HEART THAT ARE NOT FROM HIM. USE THE SPACE BELOW TO WRITE DOWN WHAT GOD REVEALS, AND ASK HIM FOR A SPIRITUAL REDIRECT.

DAY 11

# A Prayer When You Feel Discouraged

*My sheep listen to my voice; I know them, and they follow me.*
**John 10:27 (NIV)**

**YEARS AGO, ONE OF MY DAUGHTERS SAW HER BROTHER WITH A FOOTBALL TUCKED UNDER HIS ARM AND OFFERED TO THROW WITH HIM.** She hopped into place and began the game. He threw the ball, and she caught it. Then she threw the ball, and he caught it.

Back and forth they went until another voice changed the game.

"You throw weird," said one of her brothers as he passed by their game of pass and catch.

He didn't give much thought to his words, but they spoke volumes to his little sister. She sank into a spot on the steps nearby and stopped playing altogether.

But she'd missed something. Almost simultaneously with the words that discouraged her came words of affirmation and encouragement.

"Great throw!" said the brother with whom she was playing.

Two voices spoke, pointing my daughter in two very different directions. But my daughter only heard one voice.

In John chapter 10, Jesus called Himself the Good Shepherd, and we, His children, are the sheep of His pasture who can hear His voice. Jesus also confirmed that His voice was not the only voice vying for the ears of His sheep. Jesus spoke of a stranger's voice that also called to the sheep. A stranger likened to a thief who comes only to steal and kill and destroy.

Two voices pointing us in two different directions.

Based on this passage, our ability to know and hear Jesus' voice is critical to the course of our lives. It's the difference between encouraged or discouraged.

When my daughter stopped long enough to hear a different voice, one of encouragement and kindness, she jumped up from her slump and rejoined the game. This new voice changed her course completely, and the voice of the Lord will change our course too. Instead of being discouraged, we will be encouraged and equipped to take the next step with Him.

## PRAY

**Lord, help me as I learn to listen to Your voice. Give me courage to try and boldness to believe that You want to speak to me. May I not grow weary of seeking You often in quiet places. And as I do, may I follow You. In Jesus' name, Amen.**

## REFLECT

WHAT VOICES IN YOUR LIFE HAVE CONTRIBUTED TO YOU FEELING DISCOURAGED?

THINK OF THE PLACES WHERE YOU GO WHEN YOU WANT TO HEAR SOMEONE'S VOICE. IN THE SPACE BELOW, LIST SOME OF THE WAYS YOU POSITION YOURSELF WHEN YOU REALLY WANT TO HEAR SOMETHING.

HOW WILL YOU POSITION YOURSELF TODAY SO THAT THE VOICE OF THE LORD IS LOUDER THAN ANY OTHER VOICE?

DAY 12

# A Prayer When You Come to the End of Your Rope

*Then he said, "Go out and stand on the mountain in the Lord's presence." At that moment, the Lord passed by.*
**1 Kings 19:11a (CSB)**

**I SAT IN THE GROUP AND LISTENED AS MULTIPLE WOMEN SHARED.** They each had a different story, but they all arrived at the same conclusion: "I can't do this anymore!"

Maybe you know how they feel. Oftentimes our circumstances seem to push us further and further into unknown, unfamiliar, and uncomfortable places. But the women who shared these stories also shared a remarkable outcome. As they threw up their hands in distress and despair, they turned to God and He delivered them . . . not from their circumstances, but from their hopelessness.

The prophet Elijah appears to have understood this feeling, to the point he expressed to God, "I have had enough, Lord" (**1 Kings 19:4**). The following verses recount God's care of and provision for Elijah, and he obediently journeyed to the mountain of God.

Once there, God asked Elijah a question twice: "What are you doing here?"

And twice Elijah answered God with the same heavyhearted words: "I have been very zealous for the Lord God Almighty. The Israelites have rejected your covenant, torn down your altars, and put your prophets to death with the sword. I am the only one left, and now they are trying to kill me too" (**1 Kings 19:9-14**).

What I love, though, is God's response. God answered Elijah with His presence (**1 Kings 19:12a**).

I've heard it said, when you come to the end of your rope, tie a knot and hang on . . . but we don't have to hang on all alone. Just as God did for Elijah, He comforts us today with His presence. Our circumstances may not change, but God's presence in the midst of them changes us.

## PRAY

**Dear God, I know my circumstances may not always feel easy, but I'm so thankful to know I'm not alone. The next time I feel like I can't do this anymore, remind me of Your presence with me. As I turn my eyes from my circumstances to Your control, turn my hopelessness to trust. In Jesus' name, Amen.**

## REFLECT

USE THE SPACE BELOW TO BE HONEST WITH GOD ABOUT HOW YOU ARE FEELING.

HOW WILL YOU SEEK THE LORD'S PRESENCE TODAY?

## IS THERE SOMETHING YOU NEED TO DO TODAY TO BE OBEDIENT TO THE LORD'S INSTRUCTIONS?

DAY 13

# A Prayer When You Face Change You Didn't Ask For

*The Lord directs the steps of the godly.*
*He delights in every detail of their lives.*
**Psalm 37:23 (NLT)**

**I SAT IN MY CHAIR AND STARED AT THE WALL.** Just one week before, I had been overwhelmed with the blessings of my current situation. My joy had almost brought me to tears. At that moment, I never imagined that just a few days later, everything that had seemed right would suddenly be shattered into what felt like a million pieces and lead me and my family to a completely different life.

Sometimes instead of trusting God and believing He has ordered every step of our journeys, including the ones we didn't ask for, we can feel overwhelmed, afraid, or even hopeless. But when we face change we didn't ask for, we can remember that God's plans are always intentional.

God's Word confirms this over and over as we observe God lead His people. We find one example of God's intentional, yet unexpected, leading of His people in the book of Exodus:

First, God took Israel a longer way to the Promised Land so that they would not have to face a battle with the Philistines (**Exodus 13:17**). Then, God led Israel to a barren place before He took them to an oasis in order to teach them to diligently listen to His voice and prove their faithfulness to Him (**Exodus 15:22-27**).

Neither of these circumstances would have been what God's people expected or desired, but God's plans were purposeful. No matter what you face today, I pray that these verses help you see that God's ways are intentional and purposeful for you as well.

## PRAY

**Dear God, I wouldn't have planned this for myself, but I trust You. I admit I can grow anxious about what's ahead. Calm my heart with Your perfect peace. Encourage me on my journey today, and when I'm tempted to lose hope, remind me of Your loving guidance. In Jesus' name, Amen.**

## REFLECT

WHAT CHANGE ARE YOU FACING TODAY THAT YOU DIDN'T ASK FOR?

## HOW HAVE YOU FELT LIKE YOUR CIRCUMSTANCES HAVE GONE WRONG?

## HOW DO THE SOMETIMES UNEXPECTED, YET INTENTIONAL, WAYS GOD LEADS US GIVE YOU HOPE TODAY?

DAY 14

# A Prayer to Get You Ready for Whatever Comes Your Way

*The mind of man plans his way, but the Lord directs his steps.*
**Proverbs 16:9 (NASB)**

**THE CHAIRS RATTLED AS A LINE OF MEN MARCHED PAST ME.** A few minutes later, my five-year-old joined the procession with a chair of his own. To my left, a small group huddled in the hall next to a window. One man, with his Bible open, stood up front.

The lights may have been off, but the Light of the World shone bright. An evening storm had knocked out the power to the church building. Still, people gathered for worship anyway.

I laughed at the sight of my three-year-old hunched over a dirt pile next to the chairs. My daughter shed her shoes. My nine-year-old bellowed as loud as his little lungs would let him. This certainly wasn't how anyone had planned the morning to go, yet the unexpected change refreshed me in a way no ordinary service ever had.

God doesn't always let us in on His purposes, but what looks like a setback in our eyes can actually be God's perfect way of setting us up for His blessings.

Don't get me wrong, there's nothing wrong with making plans. But on the days when everything seems to go wrong, we don't have to feel unprepared. We can be sure that even when God's path looks different from our plans, He still has purpose for us.

## PRAY

**Dear God, Thank You for the truth that what surprises me never surprises You. I don't know what this day holds, but I know You do. And I know Your plans for me are good. Set me up for Your blessings today! Help me hold my plans loosely and hold fast to You, trusting You will prepare me for whatever comes my way today. In Jesus' name, Amen.**

## REFLECT

WHAT ARE YOU ANXIOUS ABOUT TODAY?

HOW DOES KNOWING THAT, IN CHRIST, YOU ARE ALWAYS PREPARED FOR WHATEVER COMES YOUR WAY, CHANGE HOW YOU APPROACH EACH DAY?

HOW WILL YOU EMBRACE WHAT FEELS LIKE A DETOUR FROM YOUR PLANS?

DAY 15

# A Prayer to Help You Release What You Don't Need

*When you go through deep waters, I will be with you.*
*When you go through rivers of difficulty, you will not drown.*
*When you walk through the fire of oppression, you will not be burned up; the flames will not consume you.*
**Isaiah 43:2 (NLT)**

DURING LUKE'S FOOTBALL CAREER, MY FAMILY AND I MOVED A DOZEN TIMES. (Literally!)

After about the fourth upheaval of all of our things, I no longer looked forward to new memories and planting roots because each new place had no more certainty than the last one. I was exhausted.

Although I knew I couldn't cling to the idea of never moving again, I determined to do it differently. One thing at a time, I whittled away at our stuff and created a simpler, much more manageable life of mobility . . . and I never missed the things we left behind.

In **Isaiah 43:2**, God promised to be with His people as they journeyed through deep waters, rivers of difficulty, and the fire of oppression. While we may never literally go through deep water or walk through fire, our daily circumstances can certainly feel that way.

Here's the thing, though—if we were literally walking through deep waters, we would leave what wasn't an absolute necessity on the bank. We wouldn't drag extra possessions into the waters with us only to weigh us down and make the journey more difficult and dangerous. Instead, we'd only carry what we need.

Instead of asking, "What do I need?" we can shift our perspective to wonder, "What *don't* I need?" As we do, God will reveal the things weighing us down and help us release them so that we can walk more freely with Him.

## PRAY

**Dear God, thank You for the promise of Your presence as I walk through each day. Show me what I'm carrying that only weighs me down. Free me up to walk faithfully and joyfully with You today. As I let go of what You show me, help me trust Your provision to give me everything I need. In Jesus' name, Amen.**

## REFLECT

LET'S APPLY THIS QUESTION TO A FEW DIFFERENT AREAS OF OUR LIVES. FIRST, CONSIDER YOUR PHYSICAL POSSESSIONS. WHAT *DON'T* YOU NEED?

NOW CONSIDER YOUR DAILY HABITS.
WHAT *DON'T* YOU NEED?

FINALLY, CONSIDER YOUR THOUGHT LIFE. WHAT *DON'T* YOU NEED TO DWELL ON OR THINK ABOUT?

DAY 16

# A Prayer When You Need Rest

*Joshua took the whole land, according to all that the Lord had spoken to Moses . . . And the land had rest from war.*
**Joshua 11:23**

**I ALWAYS LOVE A HAPPY ENDING.** The last verse of Joshua 11 communicates a bit of a "happy ending" for the nation of Israel; however, some scholars speculate that it took seven years to conquer the land. This certainly wasn't a quick and easy process. Instead, it was one that required endurance.

I've often wondered how Joshua might have felt with each new battle. Did he go more confidently into the last battle than he did the first, or did he have doubts each time a bigger, stronger army formed against him?

The Bible doesn't tell us how Joshua felt, but it does tell us what he did. Time and time again, he turned to the Lord for guidance and obeyed what He said.

This obedience positioned Israel to receive their inheritance from the Lord and ushered in the time when the land rested from war.

The day is coming when we will enter our eternal inheritance and experience perfect rest in the presence of our God and Savior. Until then, we can enjoy the blessing of the rest that comes from the assurance of our acceptance and access to His presence (**Hebrews 4:16**).

When we have doubts, when the road is hard, when the battle is long, we can persevere in faith and rejoice in knowing that our perseverance culminates in God's perfect rest.

## PRAY

**Dear God, I trust that, in You, there is a place of relief that goes far deeper than physical rest. I need the soul rest that only You can give me. Help me draw near to You even when it feels like there is too much to do. Help me turn to You over and over again and receive Your rest today no matter what I face. In Jesus' name, Amen.**

## REFLECT

WHAT ARE YOU FACING TODAY THAT STIRS UNREST IN YOUR SOUL?

WHERE DO YOU TYPICALLY TURN WHEN YOU FEEL OVERWHELMED BY THE CIRCUMSTANCES YOU LISTED ABOVE? DO YOU CALL A FRIEND? PICK UP YOUR PHONE? ENGAGE IN AN UNHEALTHY HABIT?

WHEN YOU FIND YOURSELF REACHING FOR WHATEVER YOU LISTED IN THE SPACE ABOVE, HOW CAN YOU ALLOW IT TO REDIRECT YOU INSTEAD TO THE PRESENCE OF JESUS?

DAY 17

# A Prayer When You Need Confidence

*I lift up my eyes to the hills. From where does my help come?*
*My help comes from the Lord, who made heaven and earth.*
**Psalm 121:1-2 (ESV)**

**DEFEAT TURNED HIS USUALLY BRIGHT SMILE INTO A FROWN.** "It's too hard. I can't do it," my son cried. Through his tears and protests, I assured him, "You *can* do this."

Years ago, one of my boys attempted to put together a puzzle much bigger than the one he would normally do with ease. After placing just a few pieces, I found him surveying all that was still missing. He looked defeated even before he truly began.

"I can't do one with this many pieces. I can only do the smaller ones," he protested.

Despite his lack of confidence, I was sure he'd be successful, so I encouraged him to take it one piece at a time. I suggested that he look at the matching color groups and reminded him of some things he already knew. We celebrated every step toward the finished product, and as you may have guessed, he put the puzzle together without any trouble.

With each piece he placed successfully into the puzzle, his confidence grew. By the time he pushed the last part into its place, a smile stretched across his face.

Sometimes I think life can feel a lot like my son's experience with the puzzle. The big picture of a task or the day ahead or a dream for the future overwhelms us. We attempt to figure the whole thing out all at once, and in the process, we become so defeated that we lose confidence and feel tempted to give up before we ever begin.

But the big picture belongs to God. And just like I knew with my son, God knows you can do it—even if you don't.

## PRAY

**Dear God, thank You for helping me understand that I don't have to have all the answers. Help me hear Your voice of encouragement today. Open my eyes to see Your next step and give me confidence as I take one step at a time with You. In Jesus' name, Amen.**

## REFLECT

WHAT TASK, ASSIGNMENT, OR CIRCUMSTANCE IS CAUSING YOU TO LACK CONFIDENCE?

HOW HAVE YOU TRIED TO FIGURE IT ALL OUT OR WORK IT OUT ENTIRELY INSTEAD OF SIMPLY TAKING ONE STEP AT A TIME?

WHAT SINGLE STEP WILL YOU
TAKE WITH GOD TODAY?

DAY 18

# A Prayer for the Nights You Can't Sleep

*I lie awake thinking of you, meditating on you through the night.*
*Because you are my helper, I sing for joy in the shadow of your wings.*
**Psalm 63:6-7**

**SEVERAL YEARS AGO, OUR DAUGHTER WOULD REGULARLY MAKE HER WAY TO OUR BED IN THE WEE HOURS OF THE NIGHT.** Each time, she wanted the same thing—the coveted spot in the bed between Mom and Dad. When we pulled her up and placed her between us, the cries that had accompanied her into the room ceased.

I can think of many times when I, too, have been up at night. Usually, it's because I can't turn off my thoughts, whether I'm worried about a loved one or mulling over something that needs to get done the next day.

For the nights when we can't sleep, Psalm 63 gives us a place to focus our thoughts. King David penned the words in today's verse while in the wilderness, on the run from a vast army led by his own rebellious son. If there was ever a moment to be up at night worrying, that would be it.

And David did lie awake at night, but not for the reasons we'd expect. Instead of fearing for his life or devising a plan of escape, he couldn't stop thinking about God.

The next time you lie awake at night, remember: God's up, so you don't have to be. Then shift your thoughts from your circumstances to your Savior and close your eyes. Instead of counting all the things you have to do or the problems you still need to solve, you can recall God's greatness, power, and provision.

You may even want to write the words "God's up, so I don't have to be" on a note card and put it near your bed. Read it before you go to sleep, and let it remind you to pray and praise God for His goodness.

## PRAY

**Dear God, I want my thoughts to swirl with praises to You instead of churn with anxiety. Help me shift my thoughts to the richness of Your presence and provision. As I do, bring me rest in Your presence. In Jesus' name, Amen.**

## REFLECT

USE THE SPACE BELOW TO LIST THE THINGS THAT KEEP YOU UP AT NIGHT.

NOW, MAKE A LIST OF THE WAYS YOU HAVE EXPERIENCED GOD'S FAITHFULNESS, POWER, AND PROVISION.

DAY 19

# A Prayer to Help You Smile Without Fear of the Future

*Strength and dignity are her clothing, And she smiles at the future.*
**Proverbs 31:25 (NASB)**

**HIS LITTLE BODY TREMBLED AS HE LAID HIS HEAD ON A PILLOW NEAR OUR BED.** With each flash of lightning and rumble of thunder, his eyes grew wider. He asked me if it would all be okay. He wanted me to assure him that the weather would not be severe and that it would pass without harm.

I wanted to tell him what his heart longed to hear, but the truth was, I didn't know. The forecast showed the intensity of the storms and predicted we could be in the path of the strongest cells. There was one thing, though, I was sure I could offer my son in his fear.

While I couldn't predict the weather, I knew the One who controlled it.

I pointed my son to God—His care, His control, His goodness, and His love. Although I didn't know what the future held, I knew the nature of the God who holds it, and I knew that was something sure my son could hold on to as well.

Much like my son, for years I, too, wrestled with fear . . . specifically, fear of the future. I sensed all that my fear was stealing from me. I knew my fear of the future robbed me of peace, joy, and purpose. I didn't want to continue living in fear, but I needed someone to tell me that my future wouldn't be filled with my worst-case scenarios. Of course, no one could.

But, like my son that night in the storm, as I began to turn my attention away from my fear of the future and onto my God who loves me, He taught me to live faithfully in the present and let Him handle the future.

## PRAY

**Heavenly Father, there is such unrest in the world. When I look around, it can feel so hopeless. But God, I turn to You. Help me trust You more to handle and arrange my future according to Your goodness and love. As I do, I pray You bring a smile to my face. Help me enjoy Your blessings today and look forward to the plans You have for me. In Jesus' name, Amen.**

## REFLECT

WHAT FEARS ARE KEEPING YOU FROM SMILING TODAY?

USE THE SPACE BELOW TO WRITE DOWN TRUTHS ABOUT GOD'S CHARACTER OR WAYS YOU HAVE WITNESSED HIS FAITHFULNESS IN YOUR LIFE.

DAY 20

# A Prayer to Help You Find Strength in the Lord

*My beloved brothers and sisters, be steadfast, immovable, always excelling in the work of the Lord [always doing your best and doing more than is needed], being continually aware that your labor [even to the point of exhaustion] in the Lord is not futile nor wasted [it is never without purpose].*

**1 Corinthians 15:58 (AMP)**

**CLEANING OUT CLOTHES, I FOUND A LITTLE SHIRT ALL FOUR OF MY BOYS HAD WORN AT ONE TIME OR ANOTHER.** The shirt showed its wear: torn sleeves, cracked paint, faded colors. Years and years of wear and tear had left the shirt completely worn out.

As I held the shirt in my hands, I thought of the smiles and giggles when I played peek-a-boo pulling the shirt over each little boy's head. Tears ran down my cheeks as I recalled the arms that hugged me and the little heads that had rested on my shoulder as we sang one last song before bed.

The shirt was worn out, but only because of the fullness of the lives that had been lived in it.

As I retraced the joy of each little boy and their days spent wearing the shirt, I couldn't think of even one moment of frustration—not one memory of exhaustion or feeling overwhelmed.

It's not that those times weren't there. On some of those days, I absolutely felt tired and defeated. I just didn't remember them. The blessings of that time outmatched the burdens, and my memory only absorbed the oceans of love and laughter, leaving the rest behind.

If you feel worn out today, be encouraged: Worn out isn't always a bad thing. When we feel like we don't have what it takes, God's grace is sufficient—for us, for our families, for our communities.

## PRAY

**Lord Jesus, shine Your light on me, that I may reflect it onto my children. Fill me with Your grace, that I may pour it into their hearts. Cover me with Your love that I may tuck my little ones beneath it too. Strengthen my feet that I may meet this day. In Jesus' name, Amen.**

## REFLECT

HOW HAVE YOU BELIEVED THAT FEELING WORN OUT IS A BAD THING?

HOW DOES SHIFTING YOUR PERSPECTIVE TO GOD'S SUFFICIENT GRACE ENCOURAGE YOU?

HOW WILL YOU RELY ON GOD'S GRACE TO BE SUFFICIENT IN YOUR CIRCUMSTANCES TODAY?

DAY 21

# A Prayer When You Need to Trust God with the People You Love

*You are my portion and my cup of blessing; You hold my future.*
**Psalm 16:5**

**SEVERAL YEARS AGO, WE DROPPED OUR OLDEST SON OFF AT OVERNIGHT CAMP FOR THE FIRST TIME.** I knew the camp, I knew the people, and I knew we were doing something good for our son, but my heartstrings still stretched.

We walked him to his cabin, made his bed, and lingered in his room. In fact, we stayed so long that it prompted our son to ask, "When are y'all leaving?" I took a deep breath, issued one last hug, then started the long walk to the car without my baby. As I walked, I worried.

*Who will tell him when it's time for dinner? Who will sit next to him and rub his back while he prays? Who will ask questions to be sure he's okay?*

In Psalm 16, the psalmist praised the Lord for His provision over the present and the future: *"You are my portion and my cup of blessing; You hold my future."*

This verse reminds me of the many ways I've witnessed God provide for me, bless me, and map out a future for me. As I considered God's care and provision for my life, I found peace as I realized I can trust He will do the same for my children and all those I love and pray for.

Because God is faithful and loves the people we love even more than we do, we can release them into God's care as they grow into His plans.

God is our portion. God is our blessing. God holds our futures.

## PRAY

**Dear God, I've seen You move and work so often in my own life. Help me trust that the same provision I've witnessed from Your hand is at work in the lives of those I love. Draw them nearer to You each day. May they feast on Your portion, rejoice in Your blessing, and trust in You for their future. In Jesus' name, Amen.**

## REFLECT

IN THE SPACE BELOW, WRITE DOWN THE NAMES OF THE PEOPLE YOU ARE WORRIED ABOUT TODAY AND WHY YOU ARE WORRIED ABOUT THEM.

USE THE SPACE BELOW TO RECOUNT SPECIFIC WAYS YOU HAVE SEEN GOD'S PROVISION IN YOUR PAST AND HOW IT BLESSED YOUR FUTURE.

DAY 22

# A Prayer When You're Ready for a New Start

*Get yourself ready!*
**Jeremiah 1:17a (NIV)**

**MY WRITING JOURNEY BEGAN MORE THAN A DECADE AGO, AND THE FIRST STEPS WERE NOT AT ALL WHAT I ENVISIONED.**

During my ninth month of pregnancy—with my sixth child, while my husband spent three weeks away from home for football training camp!—I felt God's nudge to attend a writer's conference.

I felt sure this was absurd and sought confirmation of these feelings from my husband. He, however, agreed with God, and without hesitation encouraged me to do it. One of God's Old Testament prophets knew the feeling. When God commissioned him, he protested, "I can't speak for you! I'm too young!" (**Jeremiah 1:6**).

Still, Jeremiah sought God personally and completely, and God took him on a bit of a practice run. Two times, God gave Jeremiah a word and asked him, "What do you see?" Both times Jeremiah saw correctly. God knew Jeremiah had what it would take.

We may be inclined to believe we play no part in preparing for God's plans, but God's words to Jeremiah told a totally different story.

If you're ready for a new start today, your first step may be to get yourself ready. You're not too young. You're not too old. Life's not too busy. You don't need more experience or training. Instead of protesting, let's prepare. Instead of arguing with God, let's trust that He will provide everything we need. Then let's take a step of faith into a new adventure with Him.

## PRAY

**Dear Heavenly Father, I want to walk with You in the plans You have prepared for me. Show me what You have given me to invest in Your Kingdom, and give me courage to do what You desire with what You have given me. I'm ready for a new start! In Jesus' name, Amen.**

## REFLECT

WHAT HAS GOD GIVEN YOU THAT YOU CAN USE FOR HIS PURPOSES?

## WHAT PRACTICAL STEPS CAN YOU TAKE TO GET READY FOR THE WAYS GOD WANTS TO USE YOU?

## WHO WILL YOU REACH OUT TO FOR ACCOUNTABILITY AND PRAYER?

DAY 23

# A Prayer When You Need Focus

*If then you have been raised with Christ, seek the things that are above, where Christ is, seated at the right hand of God.*
**Colossians 3:1 (ESV)**

**I RECENTLY READ ABOUT THE TRAINING REGIMENS OF OLYMPIC ATHLETES.** The comprehensiveness of their routines intrigued me. Olympic athletes train for the specific sport they will compete in, but preparation includes everything from maintaining optimal sleep habits to mental training to diet and hydration.

Everything they do revolves around being prepared to compete, and it is often a major change from what their life looked like before training began.

In Colossians 3:1 Paul instructed followers of Jesus to seek the things that are above. Other translations say, "Aim at and seek the [rich, eternal treasures] that are above" (**AMPC**) or "Keep seeking the things that are above" (**NASB**).

This same Greek word used in Colossians 3:1 is found in Matthew 6, where Jesus told His listeners to "seek first" God's Kingdom and righteousness (**v. 33**). Just before Jesus told them what to seek, He drew attention to some of the earthly things that can distract us—what we will eat or drink or wear (**Matthew 6:25**).

As He urged His listeners not to worry about those things, Jesus turned their attention instead to heavenly things pointing to God's love, care, and provision (**Matthew 6:26; Matthew 6:30**).

When we focus our hearts and minds on Jesus, it compels us to seek the things that are above instead of striving after the temporary, fleeting things of Earth (**2 Corinthians 5:14-15**). Like an Olympic athlete in training, we may find that we have to make changes to our daily routines, but the reward for seeking the things that are above is even greater than Olympic gold (**1 Corinthians 9:23-25**).

When we're tempted to focus on the things of Earth, we can remember the realities of heaven. And as we remain focused on eternal things, we can trust Him to handle everything else.

## PRAY

**Dear God, thank You for the freedom of life in Jesus. I want my life's aim to be the things above where You are seated. Nudge me today when my actions stray from this aim, and direct my focus back to heavenly things. In Jesus' name, Amen.**

## REFLECT

WHAT IS DISTRACTING YOU FROM SEEKING THE THINGS THAT ARE ABOVE?

WHAT CHANGES DO YOU
NEED TO MAKE TO AIM AT AND FOCUS ON
THE THINGS THAT ARE ABOVE?

DAY 24

# A Prayer When You Don't Want to Miss a Thing

*Don't worry about tomorrow, because tomorrow will worry about itself.*
**Matthew 6:34a (CSB)**

**I PUT DOWN MY PHONE AS HE EXITED THE ROOM, AND MY HEART SANK INTO MY STOMACH.** I had missed every word that had just come out of my son's mouth.

He had come into the kitchen to share a story with me, something that had happened to him that excited him and that he wanted to tell me all about. But my unnecessary and unproductive scrolling distracted me from the joy of the moment, and I hadn't even looked him in the eye. Consequently, as he shared, though my ears were present, they were not available to truly receive his words.

As God pricked my heart about all I had just missed, I put my phone down and called him back into the room. I sought forgiveness for my lack of attention and asked him to share with me once again. Without a second thought, he did, and I was so thankful for the chance at a do-over.

I was also humbled as I considered the reality that I may not always have the opportunity to get back a moment that I let pass me by.

Today's verse records Jesus speaking to our inclination to miss the moments right in front of us. With so much to do and think about, we can be tempted to always be producing or to worry, plan, or prepare for a moment yet to come, all the while missing out on the joys and the blessings right in front of us.

We may not be able to get back the moments we've missed in the past, but today we can decide that we don't want to miss one more thing!

## PRAY

**Dear God, I want to live invested in the moment right in front of me, but I sense my tendency to look ahead and worry about tomorrow. Open doors for me to connect to the people around me. Help me not impose my own "shoulds" and "supposed tos" that try to overwhelm me and push me forward. Help me slow down today to listen, smile, laugh, and take advantage of the moment right in front of me. In Jesus' name, Amen.**

## REFLECT

WHAT WORRIES ABOUT TOMORROW ARE CURRENTLY ON YOUR HEART AND MIND?

WHAT UNNECESSARY BURDENS ARE YOU CARRYING THAT ARE KEEPING YOU FROM FULLY INVESTING IN TODAY? (HINT: THEY MAY BEGIN WITH THE PHRASES "I SHOULD" OR "I'M SUPPOSED TO.")

DAY 25

# A Prayer When Your Heart Is Hurting

*Let us come boldly to the throne of our gracious God.*
*There we will receive his mercy, and we will find grace*
*to help us when we need it most.*
**Hebrews 4:16 (NLT)**

**I SIFTED THROUGH THE TOP DRAWER OF MY KITCHEN COUNTER ONE MORNING, LOOKING FOR SOMETHING I NEEDED WHILE ALSO FEELING KEENLY AWARE OF HOW DIFFICULT IT WOULD BE TO FIND.** Everyone knows how it is with the "junk drawer." It's a place where many things get dumped, and consequently, it's often more of a hassle than a help.

As I pushed all the stuff that had accumulated from one side of the drawer to the other, I began to recognize similarities between the junk drawer and our hearts. We pack them full of hurtful words or unmet desires with no real plan for what to do with them. Past failures, pains, and disappointments accumulate to the point that it becomes difficult to find anything else in our hearts that were meant to store the hope and love of Jesus.

That day in the kitchen I solved my problem with a resolution not to live like that any longer. I unloaded the entire junk drawer and spread everything across my counter. Then, I sorted through it. I tossed some things in the trash and only kept the things that would be beneficial for me and my family.

When our hearts are hurting, it may be an indication that we need to unload some things that have accumulated over time. We can bring all the things that have caused us pain to the throne of God and let Him gently help us sort through it all, releasing what we no longer need to carry so we will have room to store and enjoy His love, joy, peace, and hope.

## PRAY

**Dear God, the hurt in my heart feels so tender. Sometimes I'm afraid to open my heart and share my pain because it feels like it may hurt even more if I do. But I know my pain is safe with You. Thank You for the invitation to come boldly into Your presence to receive the healing and hope I so desperately need today. Give me courage to trust You and leave all my hurt in Your hands. In Jesus' name, Amen.**

## REFLECT

USE THE SPACE BELOW TO SHARE YOUR PAIN WITH GOD.

## WHAT DO YOU NEED TO LEAVE AT HIS THRONE OF GRACE?

HOW HAVE YOU EXPERIENCED HIS HELP WHEN YOU NEED IT MOST?

DAY 26

# A Prayer When You Feel the Pressure of Keeping It All Together

*All glory to God, who is able, through his mighty power at work within us, to accomplish infinitely more than we might ask or think.*
**Ephesians 3:20 (NLT)**

**MOST EVERY NIGHT, ONE OF MY KIDS STARTS HIS PRAYER LIKE THIS: "DEAR GOD, THANK YOU FOR THIS DAY."**

One night, God used his words to show me that my heart didn't overflow with thanks. My heart felt defeated, very much aware of everything I hadn't managed to do that day. My mind retraced my failures and shortcomings, and then those thoughts gave way to discouragement.

It's easy to finish a day and filter everything through the lens of perfection. We sift through every moment and focus on where we got it wrong. But instead of cataloging all of the things we *didn't* do, let's thank God for everything He *did* do.

Instead of feeling guilty for not having a house as clean as we think it should be, let's say thank You to God for a meal shared around the table.

When we're tempted to worry about future threats that could impact our loved ones, let's say thank You to God for the smiles that surround us today.

Instead of keeping a record book of our perceived failures and successes, let's say thank You to God for the strength to participate in His work today.

God's purposes are not always our own. And what He calls success may not look anything like our plans, but Ephesians 3:20 reminds us that God is able to accomplish infinitely more than we might ask or think.

## PRAY

**Dear God, I have so much to be thankful for. Forgive me for not saying thank You for all of the ways You provide for me each day. I know that Your mercies are new every morning and Your grace is sufficient for today. Alert me when I try to do it all myself. Open my eyes to see all that You are doing around me. In Jesus' name, Amen.**

## REFLECT

WHAT ARE YOU TRYING TO KEEP TOGETHER?

HOW HAVE YOU SEEN GOD'S ACTIVITY IN THE CIRCUMSTANCES YOU LISTED ABOVE?

IN THE SPACE BELOW, LIST A FEW THINGS YOU ARE THANKFUL FOR.

**DAY 27**

# A Prayer When You Need Stability

*Look! The virgin will conceive a child! She will give birth to a son, and they will call him Immanuel, which means "God is with us."*
**Matthew 1:23 (NLT)**

**ONE CHRISTMAS YEARS AGO, WE HAD RECENTLY ADOPTED A CAT, AND OUR KIDS WERE FAR MORE EAGER TO GREET OUR NEW CAT THAN HE WAS TO GET TO KNOW THEM.** The cat sought shelter in the Christmas tree, but the kids pursued him anyway, and consequently the once-glowing tree crashed into shambles on the ground.

And the truth is, it left so much more than a mess.

The truth is, when the Christmas tree tumbled that year, it took my heart with it. Life had felt especially uncertain. I felt tired and lonely. As we hung ornaments that year, I hung my heart with them because the tree represented something stable.

In its branches, it held the newlyweds tucked in for a long Ohio winter. It shared the news from when God added our first baby boy to the family. It was adorned with a Santa who clearly liked to play football, and the faces of six little ones who God sent to add wonder and thrills to each day. And every year for a decade, no matter where we lived, we lifted the same star atop this storied tree.

Then the tree came tumbling down. The water drained out, ornaments broke, pine needles scattered everywhere. The once-stable star lay separated and alone.

I sat encircled by brokenness and disappointment. But, in the midst of our mess, God redirected my weary heart to the truth: God is the certainty. God is our stability. And God is with us.

Something tells me I'm not the only one who's felt lonely or weary or heartbroken. There will be messes, and we may feel alone, but we will never be alone because Jesus is Immanuel—God with us. And we can always hang our hearts on that. He is something stable. He is something certain.

## PRAY

**Dear God, what relief I have in knowing You never change and You never waver. Show me anything unstable that I am trying to cling to today, and help me trust that You are all I need. When I feel lonely or tired, draw my heart to the truth that You are with me in every moment, no matter what I face. In Jesus' name, Amen.**

## REFLECT

WHAT FEELS UNCERTAIN OR UNSTABLE IN YOUR LIFE TODAY?

HOW CAN YOU HOLD ON TO
THE CERTAINTY OF CHRIST AND STAND
ON HIS FIRM FOUNDATION?

DAY 28

# A Prayer When You Don't Know What to Do Next

*Thy word is a lamp unto my feet, and a light unto my path.*
**Psalm 119:105 (KJV)**

ON UNFAMILIAR ROADS, I FOUND MYSELF DRIVING IN A DOWNPOUR. My hands gripped the steering wheel. My eyes shifted back and forth as I tried to keep my car inside the lane.

My husband observed my tense state and calmly instructed, "Just watch the car in front of you," he said. "As long as you go where he goes, you'll be okay."

His plan seemed too simple. I squeezed the wheel tighter and tried to watch the car in front of me. The rain hit the windshield so hard I could barely make it out, but the taillights glowed just enough for me to follow.

We've all likely experienced circumstances that felt like blinding rain under dark skies as we traverse unfamiliar roads. In times like these, we may be inclined to let our eyes focus on our circumstances, when all we have to do is watch the One in front of us.

God gave us His words and revealed His heart to us. When we don't know what to do next, we can open God's Word and do what it says. Maybe it will feel completely unrelated to what we're facing, but we can be confident that obedience to God is always the right next step.

## PRAY

**Dear God, this is so much bigger than I am. There is nothing I can do or say that will fix this or change anything. I need You. Help me trust You even when I can't see You. Help me have faith even when the light of Your love feels faint. Guide me where I need discernment and instruction. Give me rest and support in the places I am weary. Let my heart turn to You, not just in despair, but in expectation of experiencing Your goodness, kindness, power, and provision. In Jesus' name, Amen.**

## REFLECT

WHERE ARE YOUR EYES FOCUSED AS YOU TRY TO DISCERN WHAT TO DO NEXT?

WHAT IS ONE THING YOU CAN DO
DIFFERENTLY TODAY SO THAT YOU FIX YOUR EYES
ON JESUS AND NOT ON OTHER THINGS?

DAY 29

# A Prayer When You Need God to Fill Your Cup

*. . . striving with His power and energy, which so greatly works within me.*

**Colossians 1:29 (AMP)**

**FOR MANY YEARS, A FEW OF MY CHILDREN WOULD ASK ME TO LIE DOWN AND PRAY WITH THEM AT BEDTIME EACH NIGHT.** One night, as I joined them in their room, one child in particular had made a place for me.

He had scooted himself all the way over against the wall to make a spot in the bed for me. He even found an extra pillow! He had prepared room for me.

This scene took my thoughts to the lyrics of a familiar Christmas song: *Let every heart prepare Him room.*

My son prepared room for me for a few reasons. My presence brought him comfort and peace. The time I spent with him before he drifted off to sleep delighted him and filled his heart. He looked forward to it and wanted to make sure nothing got in the way of our time together.

On the days when it feels like our souls are running on empty, let's remember that nothing in this world will satisfy us. Instead of looking for something temporary in hopes it will fulfill us, let's purpose to prepare room in our hearts for Jesus, Who is the stream of Living Water that never runs dry (**John 4:13-14**).

When we do, I believe we will trade stress for a smile and experience souls overflowing with God's power and energy.

## PRAY

**Dear God, thank You for Your faithfulness that fills me up. I want to live in the fullness of Your plans for me. It's hard not to try and fix things or figure them out. Help me make room for You and abide in You today, depending on You alone for everything I need. In Jesus' name, Amen.**

## REFLECT

WHEN YOU FEEL EMPTY AND EXHAUSTED, WHAT ARE YOU INCLINED TO TURN TO INSTEAD OF GOD?

WHAT IS ONE THING YOU CAN PRACTICALLY DO TO RELY ON GOD'S POWER AND ENERGY INSTEAD OF YOUR OWN?

## HOW WILL YOU MAKE ROOM FOR JESUS TODAY?

DAY 30

# A Prayer to Help You Experience the Fullness of Christ

*Give all your worries and cares to God, for he cares about you.*
**1 Peter 5:7 (NLT)**

**I FILL MY COFFEE MAKER WITH WATER EVERY DAY.** Each time I do, I notice a line with two words beside it that reads "max fill." To be honest, I'm not sure what happens if you cross the line. I've tried really hard not to cross the line because I definitely do *not* want to mess up my morning coffee.

I wonder if sometimes we don't treat God like my coffee maker. We feel like there's a limit—a line we shouldn't cross. We think it might be okay to ask God for some things or to seek Him sometimes, but we don't believe He's interested in us coming to Him anytime to talk about everything.

We silently rank our cares based on what we think is or is not important to God, but God's love, joy, peace, and complete satisfaction are not found in a container that can be filled too high. Every time we need God, He's there. We can never ask too much, talk too much, or need too much.

God wants to hear from you today. Your cares are His cares. It's never too small or too often, and you will never reach capacity in His riches. There's no "max fill" with God. You can always receive more from His Word and in His presence.

## PRAY

**Dear Lord, I seek You today, bringing You the whole of the cares of my heart. As I look to You, let me experience Your goodness and trust Your promise to take care of me. In Jesus' name, Amen.**

# REFLECT

## WHAT ARE YOU TRYING TO HANDLE ON YOUR OWN?

USE THE SPACE BELOW TO TALK
TO GOD ABOUT EVERYTHING IN
YOUR HEART AND ON YOUR MIND.

DAY 31

# A Prayer to Help You Flourish

*How joyful are those who fear the Lord—*
*all who follow his ways! You will enjoy the fruit of your labor.*
*How joyful and prosperous you will be!*
**Psalm 128:1-2 (NLT)**

**WE ADMIRED ITS BEAUTY AS WE DROVE BY.** For a few days, we had watched what appeared to be a beautiful bloom appear on the road near our house. Upon closer observation, however, we determined this was not a beautiful bloom at all, but instead a giant weed that had gone unattended and now threatened to choke out any real flower trying to emerge.

That day, I realized how easily a counterfeit blossom can resemble the real thing.

Today's verse paints the image of a flourishing life rooted in Christ. However, just like a weed in the field can fool us at times, we can also be fooled by spiritual counterfeit flourishing.

Often, we believe the path to flourishing includes what we can get and how much of it we can keep, but God's Word simplifies a joyous and prosperous life into two steps: Fear the Lord and follow His ways. (The verse actually includes an exclamation point!)

To fear the Lord is not to be afraid of Him. Instead, it is actually a concept of intimacy—the kind of intimacy with God that leads to a flourishing, abundant life. Flourishing in the world will never prove satisfying in the way flourishing in Christ will. To seek a life that flourishes is to seek the Lord who came so that we would have life in abundance (**John 10:10**).

## PRAY

**Dear God, I long to walk in Your ways and obey You in every area of my life. Lead me to be the person You designed me to be. Forgive me for resisting complete and total surrender to You. Teach me to revere You so that I will be a fruitful vine in home, work, and community. In Jesus' name, Amen.**

## REFLECT

HOW HAVE YOU LOOKED FOR A LIFE THAT FLOURISHES APART FROM FOLLOWING GOD'S WAYS?

WHAT IS ONE THING YOU NEED
TO SURRENDER TODAY IN ORDER TO
FLOURISH AND FIND JOY IN CHRIST?

REREAD PSALM 128:1-2. USE THE SPACE BELOW TO DESCRIBE HOW YOUR HEART FEELS AS YOU CONSIDER A LIFE THAT FLOURISHES IN CHRIST.

DAY 32

# A Prayer to Calm Your Thoughts

*Do not be conformed to this age, but be transformed by the renewing of your mind, so that you may discern what is the good, pleasing, and perfect will of God.*
**Romans 12:2 (CSB)**

**A FEW YEARS AGO, MY HUSBAND, LUKE, DECIDED TO COVER THE WALLS OF OUR HOUSE WITH WOOD PANELING.** From the ceiling to the floor, he cut, sanded, stained, and installed one wood plank after another. It completely transformed the appearance of our living space.

Recently a friend of mine came over to visit, and as she surveyed the floor-to-ceiling boards, she wondered, "Katy, what was here before?"

She had visited my house before the wood boards went up, but now she couldn't remember what the wall used to look like.

I heard a pastor speak about Scripture in a similar sense. He said:

*Let Scripture be the wallpaper of your mind.*

Like the boards Luke lined each wall of our home with, when the walls of our minds are covered in Scripture, it completely changes us. Instead of bouncing back and forth from one desperate headline to another, our thoughts are anchored in truth. Instead of bearing the scratches and stains of sin, our minds are covered by God's grace, goodness, faithfulness, power, and provision.

Don't get me wrong, our home renovation took time. It was a tedious process, as any wallpaper project is, but even in the process, the transformation was easy to see and only caused us to look forward to the finished project.

To calm your thoughts today, simply start by laying the first board of Scripture in your mind. Then one day at a time, lay another piece of Scripture until Scripture is the wallpaper of your mind.

## PRAY

**Dear God, the world feels so loud, but I don't want to be tossed around with every new reason to worry. I know Your Word tells me not to be anxious but to pray with thanksgiving, so that is what I will do right now. Thank You that I can approach Your throne of grace anytime about anything. I pray that You will work in the circumstances that swirl around me. Calm the chaos. Quiet the storm and let the peace of Christ rule in my heart. In Jesus' name, Amen.**

## REFLECT

WHAT WOULD YOU SAY IS CURRENTLY THE WALLPAPER OF YOUR MIND?

WHAT IS ONE WAY YOU CAN
REPLACE THE CURRENT WALLPAPER OF
YOUR MIND WITH SCRIPTURE?

DAY 33

# A Prayer to Remind You That God Sees You

*You know when I sit and when I rise;*
*you perceive my thoughts from afar. You discern my going out*
*and my lying down; you are familiar with all my ways.*
**Psalm 139:2-3 (NIV)**

**SEVERAL YEARS AGO, I FOUND MYSELF IN A TOUGH PLACE.** As I settled into a new neighborhood and new routines, I felt overwhelmed and alone. I knew God's promises about how He'd never leave me, but I still woke up each day afraid.

In one desperate moment, I prayed, "God, please tell someone to pray for me. Put me on someone's heart. Tell them I need them to intercede for me."

Months later, I passed by a new friend. I had met her around the same time I was struggling through each day. We never really hung out, and our conversations were usually short, but she was a sweet person, and I always enjoyed bumping into her.

This particular day, she told me how, after the very first day we met, God put me on her heart, and she had prayed for me regularly.

When I begged God to put me on someone's heart, I imagined the faces of family and friends who thought of me often. I never imagined that an acquaintance I barely knew would be the one God chose to answer my prayers.

God is at work even when we don't see it or feel it. He is familiar with all of our ways. The original Hebrew word translated as "familiar" communicates the idea of being intimately acquainted with something or someone.

Not only is God familiar with all of our ways, the same God who searched our hearts and knows us has given us the Holy Spirit who pleads for us before Him (**Psalm 139:1, Romans 8:27**). Though we may not always feel it, we can be certain God is active all around us, working things out in ways we couldn't even imagine.

## PRAY

**Dear God, I'm humbled today as I consider that even as I offer up this prayer, You see me and hear my cry. I'm so thankful I can count on You to work in my circumstances on my behalf and for my good. Help me bring my cares to You and confidently trust You to take up my cause. In Jesus' name, Amen.**

## REFLECT

WHAT CIRCUMSTANCES HAVE MADE YOU FEEL LIKE GOD DOESN'T SEE YOU OR DOESN'T CARE?

HOW DOES KNOWING HE NOT ONLY SEES YOU BUT HE IS INTIMATELY ACQUAINTED WITH EVERYTHING YOU DO GIVE YOU HOPE TODAY?

ASK GOD TO PUT SOMEONE'S NAME ON YOUR HEART. WRITE THEIR NAME HERE, AND MAYBE EVEN WRITE OUT A PRAYER FOR THEM, THEN PRAY FOR THEM OFTEN, TRUSTING GOD IS AT WORK.

DAY 34

# A Prayer When You Feel Like You're Running on Empty

*He [the Lord] satisfies the longing soul,*
*and the hungry soul he fills with good things.*
**Psalm 107:9 (ESV)**

## HOW ARE YOU?

If you're anything like me, your instinctive response to that question goes something like, "I'm fine."

I once observed someone pose this question to a group of ladies, and I loved how one woman responded: "We're doing fine!" she said. "You know what they say *fine* means: frustrated, irritated, neurotic, emotional."

What I loved the most about this statement is that the woman who said it is a wise, godly woman who has lived her life for the cause of Christ. In her wisdom, she didn't try to pretend her life was absent of frustration or difficulty. Instead, she was honest about her circumstances.

It's important for us to recognize when we're running on empty. Just like when a car runs low on gasoline or a cell phone's battery is about to run out, our hearts, souls, and minds give us indicators that we're getting low on spiritual fuel. These "warning lights" may be different for each of us, but when we learn to identify them, we can take the proper next step.

Once we acknowledge our limits, the necessary next step is to be honest about our need to fill up. When our cell phone alerts us to a lower battery, we often waste no time finding a charging cord. Many times, we bring that charging cord with us wherever we go.

If only we will treat the fullness of our souls the same way. Satisfaction for a longing soul is always available. All we have to do is turn to Jesus and let Him fill us with good things.

## PRAY

**Heavenly Father, for so long I've lived with a soul running on empty. I don't want to live one more day like that. I believe You can and will satisfy my longing soul. Oh, how I desire the good things You have for me today. Alert me to my soul's low-fuel indicators, and show me the necessary next steps to fill up in Your presence. In Jesus' name, Amen.**

## REFLECT

WHAT ARE SOME INDICATORS THAT YOUR SOUL IS RUNNING ON EMPTY?

HOW DO YOU NORMALLY
HANDLE THESE INDICATORS?

WHAT IS ONE NECESSARY STEP YOU WILL TAKE TO LET GOD SATISFY YOUR LONGING SOUL?

DAY 35

# A Prayer When You're Trying to Trust God More

*Trust in the Lord with all your heart, and do not lean on your own understanding. In all your ways acknowledge him, and he will make straight your paths.*
**Proverbs 3:5-6 (ESV)**

**RECENTLY, ONE OF MY FAVORITE PASTIMES HAS BECOME WALKING WITH MY TWO DOGS.** We are surrounded by wide-open spaces, so when we walk, my dogs don't have to be on a leash. Of my two pups, one is older and walks at a slower pace, usually near my side. The other, however, is much younger with much more energy, and she often grows weary of my pace.

As she waits—not so patiently—for me to keep her with her, she usually runs way ahead of me. Eventually she stops and turns around to watch where I go. If I turn down a road different from the one she took, she runs back to where I am so she can take the path I walked instead of the one she had begun.

She doesn't like to wait on me, but she does like to walk with me.

Sometimes I think we treat our relationship with God the same way. We want His path and believe it is good for us, but when we can't quite see how He is working, or when His plans seem to take longer than we'd like, we run ahead and try to make our own way instead of trusting God and His way.

Our own understanding will fail us. It is limited and flawed. But we can always trust the paths of our Savior. When we find ourselves growing impatient or anxious, instead of running ahead and trying to forge our own way, we can simply choose to be obedient right where we are and wait on Jesus' next step.

## PRAY

**Dear God, I find it hard sometimes to slow down. It feels uncomfortable to wait. I want to follow You, but I admit I also want to know where we're going. I want to trust You more even when I don't understand. Help me today to find more satisfaction in simply walking with You. In Jesus' name, Amen.**

## REFLECT

WHAT DO YOU FIND IT HARD TO TRUST GOD WITH?

## HOW HAVE YOU LEANED ON YOUR UNDERSTANDING?

WHAT IS ONE THING YOU CAN DO TODAY TO ACKNOWLEDGE GOD IN ALL YOUR WAYS?

DAY 36

# A Prayer When You're Tired of Carrying the Weight of Your Worry

*The LORD will fight for you; you need only to be still.*
**Exodus 14:14 (NIV)**

**EVERY TIME I MAKE SPAGHETTI, I BURN A RIM OF HARDENED SAUCE AROUND THE DISH.** I've tried sponges and brushes and a little bit of elbow grease, and no matter what I try, they all end up with the same result: Eventually my arm tires, and I call it quits.

Consequently, I developed a new strategy. Instead of scrubbing, I put the soap straight into the dish and turn on the faucet. I watch as the dish disappears beneath a sea of soap suds. Then, I walk away.

After a while, I return to find the suds simmered down and beginning to take on the color of the dish. I dump the dirty water down the drain, run a little more hot water through the pan and, *voilà*!

No sponge. No scrubbing. No problem. Without any help from my hand, the dish sparkles clean.

Sometimes my heart can mirror my spaghetti dish. My cares and concerns cake around the edges, and it takes everything I have to chip away at the buildup. I wrestle. I worry. I walk around weighed down.

No matter how hard I fight to point myself in the right direction, I can't seem to release the weight of even one worry.

It may be that the most radical way we can get rid of the burdens in our hearts is to be still—walk away from our own efforts and turn straight toward the presence of God.

Let's take a few minutes right now, at this moment, to stop scrubbing. Say out loud or whisper silently the things caked heavy on your heart. Then sit still with God and let Him fight for you.

## PRAY

**Dear Heavenly Father, I'm so tired of carrying these burdens and fears. I've tried everything to overcome them, and I admit I cannot do it on my own. I can't fix it or figure it out. I believe that in my stillness You are strong. Do for me what I cannot do for myself. In Jesus' name, Amen.**

## REFLECT

USE THE SPACE BELOW TO WRITE DOWN THE WORRIES THAT ARE WEIGHING YOU DOWN.

## HOW DO YOU FEEL WHEN YOU CONSIDER BEING STILL AND LETTING GOD FIGHT FOR YOU?

## HOW WILL YOU INTENTIONALLY ALLOW GOD TO CARRY YOUR BURDENS TODAY?

DAY 37

# A Prayer When You're Still Waiting

*Who would have said to Abraham that Sarah would nurse a baby? Yet I have given Abraham a son in his old age!*
**Genesis 21:7 (NLT)**

**FOR MUCH OF MY LIFE, I'VE HAD A FAVORITE FOUR-WORD EXPRESSION: I TOLD YOU SO!** (Somewhere my mom and sister are nodding their heads profusely.)

Oh, how I loved to predict the outcome of a situation then utter my favorite four words when it all went the way I said it would. If I'm honest, I probably thought I had it all figured out . . . then I grew up. And as I grew older, life grew bigger.

A life that once seemed fairly foreseeable became more and more uncertain. Unwelcome surprises caught me off guard, and what I thought I had all figured out became impossible for me to predict.

My life felt out of control. I no longer boasted about what I thought I knew. Instead, I grasped for something certain.

That's when God taught me a new four-word expression.

Genesis 21 begins with words of great hope and assurance, "The Lord kept his word and did for Sarah exactly what he had promised" (**Genesis 21:1**). But the promise God fulfilled to Sarah and Abraham had been twenty-five years in the making! On top of that, Sarah's childbearing years had come and gone . . . she was ninety years old when she gave birth to Isaac.

The Bible records Sarah's response: "Who would have said to Abraham that Sarah would nurse a baby? Yet I have given Abraham a son in his old age!" (**Genesis 21:7**). And it's here that we find my new favorite four-word expression: Who would have said!

We may not be able to predict how God will work things out, but we can pray it out and trust while we wait. He is at work.

## PRAY

**Heavenly Father, sometimes it feels easier to want You to show me exactly how things will go. But I know You desire me to have faith. Increase my faith today and help me look forward to the day when I, like Sarah, can exclaim, "Who would have said!" In Jesus' name, Amen.**

## REFLECT

WHAT ARE YOU WAITING FOR TODAY?

HOW HAVE YOU APPROACHED YOUR CIRCUMSTANCES TRYING TO FIGURE IT OUT INSTEAD OF PRAYING IT OUT?

HOW CAN YOU SHIFT YOUR FOCUS FROM WHAT YOU WANT TO KNOW TO ANTICIPATION FOR WHAT GOD IS DOING?

DAY 38

# A Prayer to Help You Participate in God's Plans Today

*You shall take possession of the land and settle in it, for I have given the land to you to possess it.*
**Numbers 33:53 (ESV)**

**I STOOD GUARD AT THE DOOR ON HIGH ALERT.**

With hundreds of women gathered inside, I knew exactly what I had to do. The peace of the room rested in my hands. And my hands rested securely on the door handle.

As a staff member at a women's conference, one of my assignments was to serve as the hostess of a workshop. My responsibilities included prepping the room for the workshop, assisting the speaker when she arrived, and keeping the room distraction-free.

I took my post at the door, and a sense of ownership enveloped me. I surveyed the space assigned to me and made mental notes of the empty seats so I could direct latecomers that way. Then I turned my ear to the slightest touch of the door.

The room became *my* room, *my* space to care for, *my* assignment to carry out. At that moment, I wondered about how many past assignments I'd failed to own.

In today's verse, God's people found themselves on the edge of the land God had promised them, yet they still had to "take possession of the land and settle in it."

Forty years before this, all but two men had looked at their God-given land and said, "We can't go up against them! They are stronger than we are!"

(**Numbers 13:31, NLT**). And all of those who said "we can't" lost the opportunity to possess the land.

Let's not forfeit God's gifts and special assignments on account of uncertainty or distraction. Today, let's ask God to show us the space He has given us. Then let's walk confidently in the plans that Jesus has prepared for us.

## PRAY

**Heavenly Father, what a joy it is to know You have planned good works in advance for me to do. I want to walk in them today. When I feel insecure, remind me it is You who works in me to fulfill Your good purposes. Let me not be distracted by fears or burdens that are not mine to carry. In Jesus' name, Amen.**

## REFLECT

HOW HAVE INSECURITIES INFLUENCED YOUR WILLINGNESS TO PARTICIPATE IN GOD'S PLANS?

WHAT FEARS OR CARES OF THIS WORLD MAY BE DISTRACTING YOU FROM GOD'S PLANS FOR YOU?

## WHAT IS ONE WAY YOU CAN TAKE OWNERSHIP OF YOUR GOD-GIVEN ASSIGNMENTS TODAY?

DAY 39

# A Prayer When Everything Feels Like It's Falling Apart

*My God will meet all your needs according to the riches of his glory in Christ Jesus.*
**Philippians 4:19 (NIV)**

**IN THE MIDST OF ONE OF THE MOST DIFFICULT SEASONS OF MY ADULT LIFE, I LEARNED A PRAYER FROM MY BABY GIRL.** My father had recently passed away, and the entire world had changed in the wake of a worldwide pandemic.

Everything felt like it was falling apart. It was hard to find words to pray. That's when the words of my youngest daughter rang in my ears: "God, please help Mom not be sad."

What struck me was how simple it was. She didn't follow her request with a list of ideas for how God could help me. She didn't repeat herself, pleading with God in case He hadn't heard her the first time. She asked with a sincere heart, and her trust in God's provision was enough.

She believed God heard her, understood her, and knew exactly how to help.

If you're like me, sometimes when you pray it can feel like you need to articulate specifically and clearly what you need. It can even feel like the longer you pray, the more likely you are to receive. Certainly, long prayers aren't wrong, but in this case I was impacted by my daughter's short ones.

I know you likely have many things weighing heavy on your heart. And while I don't know every detail of your needs, God does. So today I pray that my daughter's prayer will encourage you. God doesn't need your best words. He doesn't need your clearest appeal. He knows your heart. He knows what you need, and He loves you.

## PRAY

**Dear Heavenly Father, here is my heart. I know You see me. I know You hear me. I believe You know what to do and will give me everything I need. Please help me. In Jesus' name, Amen.**

## REFLECT

WHAT DO YOU NEED GOD TO HELP YOU WITH TODAY?

USE THE SPACE BELOW TO WRITE WHAT YOU NEED IN A PRAYER AS SIMPLE AS MY DAUGHTER'S. DON'T FEEL LIKE YOU NEED TO EXPLAIN YOURSELF OR ADD DETAILS. SIMPLY ASK GOD FOR WHAT YOU NEED.

HOW WILL YOU TRUST GOD'S PROVISION
AND ABILITY TO MEET YOUR NEEDS?

DAY 40

# A Prayer When You Need a Reason to Celebrate

*Let it remind you always to recite this teaching of the Lord:*
*"With a strong hand, the Lord rescued you from Egypt."*
**Exodus 13:9 (NLT)**

**IN EXODUS 13, GOD HAD MIRACULOUSLY RESCUED HIS PEOPLE OUT OF SLAVERY IN EGYPT.** After leading them to freedom, God instructed His people to celebrate annually in remembrance of what He had done for them. God called the annual festival a "visible sign . . . like a mark branded" on their hands or foreheads.

God knew the further His people traveled from the moment He delivered them from Egypt, the easier it would become for them to grumble, complain, and doubt. (And they did!) So He commanded them to count their blessings and keep His faithfulness, power, and control over all things at the forefront of their minds.

The same God who led the Israelites out of Egypt called us out of darkness and into His marvelous light (**1 Peter 2:9**). And like Israel, when we remember God's promises and recall His faithfulness, we always have something to celebrate.

It may be something as simple as God giving you a happy baby when all the other kids needed baths. Celebrate it!

Maybe a tank of gas lasted miles and miles longer than it ever should have. Celebrate it!

Maybe you asked for a last-minute babysitter and God provided. Celebrate it!

Or maybe your whole world fell apart and God pieced (or is starting to piece) it back together with His gentle, patient hand. Celebrate it!

As we choose to remember God's past faithfulness, it will lead us to a future built on His promises.

## PRAY

**Dear Lord, I don't want to spend one more minute grumbling and complaining. You have given me so much to celebrate! Bring to mind all the ways You have shown up in my life, and help me keep Your faithfulness always before me. In Jesus' name, Amen.**

## REFLECT

WHERE HAVE YOU SEEN GOD'S FAITHFULNESS IN YOUR LIFE?

## HOW WILL YOU CELEBRATE GOD'S PAST FAITHFULNESS?

# About the Author

**Katy McCown** is the author of *She Smiles without Fear: Proverbs 31 for Every Woman* and *She Belongs: Finding Your Place in the Body of Christ*. She is wife to former NFL quarterback Luke McCown, a writer for Proverbs 31 Ministries, a national speaker, and President of She Laughs Ministries. She's also the host of the *Best Day Ever* podcast and the mom of six children ranging in age from grade school to college.